Thank you for your purchase!

I ask that you please not share, modify, or resell any part of this workbook. Please direct your colleagues to our Amazon or Teachers Pay Teachers storefront. Thank you in advance for respecting the time and effort I put into creating these workbooks.

Ms. Daniela

Your purchase supports our classrooms and our families.
If you are happy with your order, please leave us a review on our Amazon storefront.

Connect with us on instagram @montessoriworkbook. We love to hear feedback and ideas for new workbooks!

MW00903695

Maria Montessori knew that for children to grow into adults who protect our planet and each other, they must first deeply understand the world around them. The Science & Geography curriculum is the foundation for the Montessori Peace Curriculum. As children study the essential role of plants, the uniqueness of other cultures and the magic of the physical world, they develop a connection and sense of responsibility for the world around them.

Language comprehension is an essential skill for your child's reading ability. In order for children to find meaning in texts they must first have a broad understanding of different subjects. The Montessori Science & Geography Curriculum was developed to support the child's background knowledge and vocabulary development.

Some of the subjects in this book may seem challenging for a young child. However, these lessons are enjoyed by even the youngest students in our 3 – 6 Montessori classroom. I invite you to explore the concepts alongside your child. Use descriptive language and most importantly, play! Search for materials around your house to experiment with, enjoy the music from different continents and go outside to find all the different shapes in nature.

Table of Contents

email *ms.danielaemontessoriworkbook.com* for a pdf. copy of all the flags from each continent.

Living vs. Non Living

Does it **breathe**?

Does it **reproduce**?

Does it **eat** food and **drink** water?

Can it **move** on its own?

 living

 non-living

blank page for cut and paste purposes ☺

Cut and paste each image in the correct category.

Living vs. Non Living

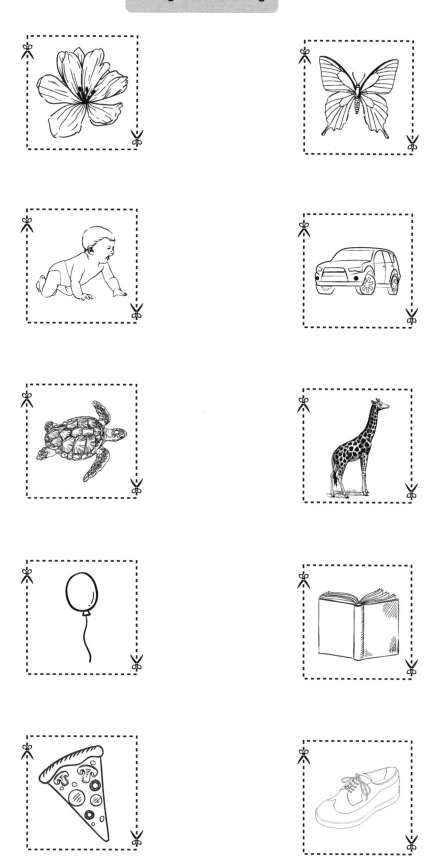

blank page for cut and paste purposes ☺

Circle all of the Living Things.

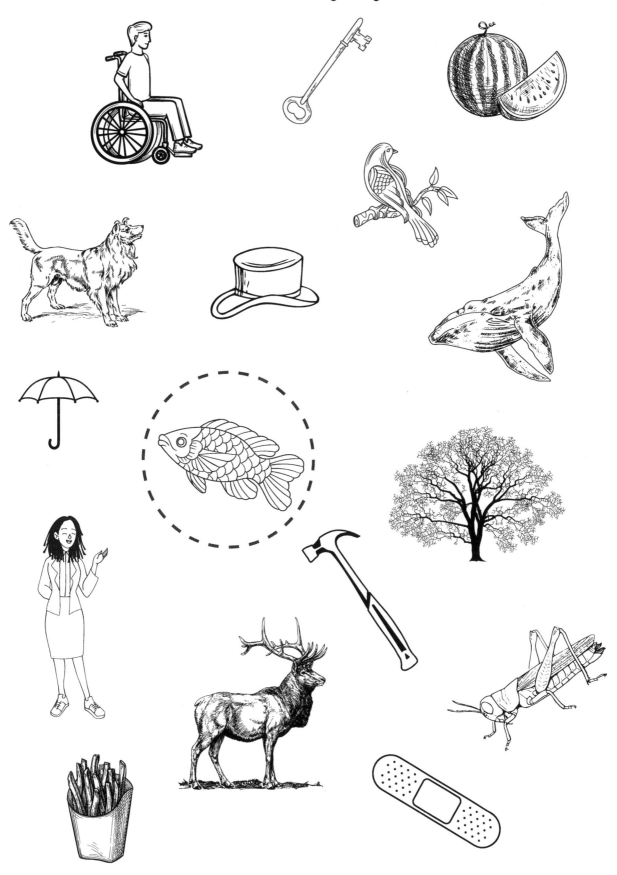

Circle all of the Non Living Things.

Plant vs. Animal

Plants and Animals are the **two main types of living things.**

Plants breathe carbon dioxide. Plants make their own food from sunlight, chlorophyll and carbon dioxide.

Animals breathe oxygen. Animals do not make their own food. They seek food sources outside their body.

 plant

 animal

7

blank page for cut and paste purposes ☺

Cut and paste each image in the correct category.

Plant vs. Animal

blank page for cut and paste purposes ☺

Circle all of the Plants.

Circle all of the Animals.

land

water

air

blank page for cut and paste purposes ☺

Cut and paste each image in the correct category.

Land, Water & Air

blank page for cut and paste purposes ☺

Land & Water Forms

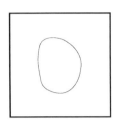

<u>Island</u> – A landform that is surrounded by water and that is much smaller than a continent.

<u>Lake</u> – A body of water that is surrounded by land and that is larger than a pond and smaller than an ocean or a sea.

<u>Bay</u> – A body of water that is partially enclosed by land with a wide opening to the ocean.

<u>Cape</u> – sliver of land that is just into the ocean and is surrounded by water on three sides.

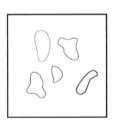

<u>Archipelago:</u> group of islands that are located close together in a body of water. They are also known as an island chain.

<u>System of lakes</u> – is a group of lakes that are located close together across a piece of land.

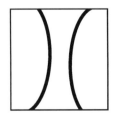

<u>Strait</u> – is a narrow passage of water connecting two large bodies of water.

<u>Isthmus</u> – is a narrow strip of land connecting two large pieces of land.

Color in the Land & Water forms and trace their names.

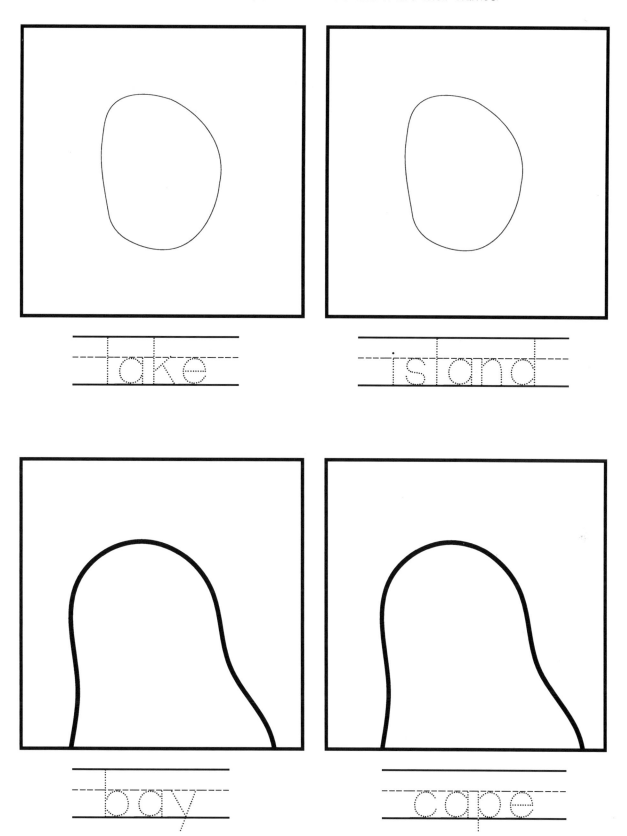

lake

island

bay

cape

14

Color in the Land & Water forms and trace their names.

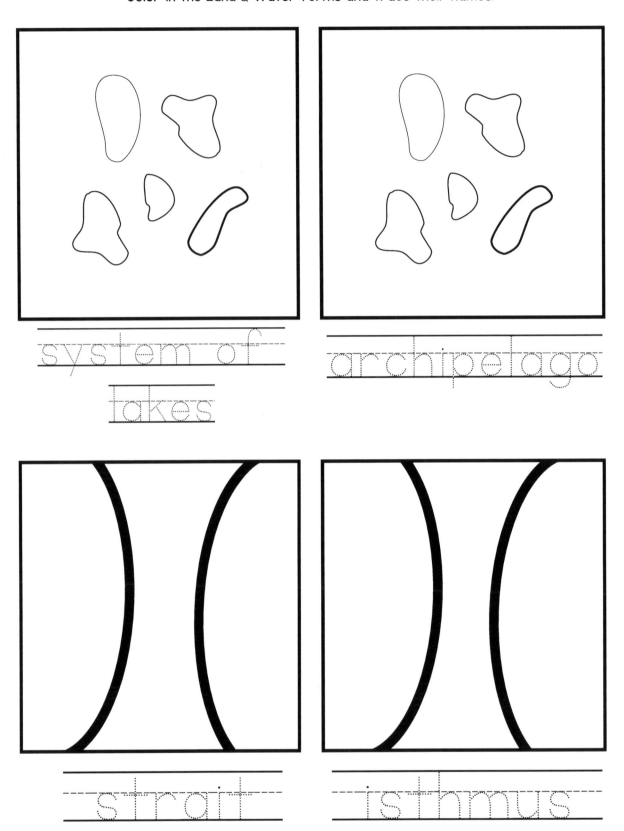

system of
lakes

archipelago

strait

isthmus

Sink vs. Float

Buoyancy is an object's ability to float in water. Whether or not an object will float depends on the amount of water an object **displaces** and the **density** of an object. Density is how close together the molecules of a substance are or how much mass a substance has in a given space.

sink	float

blank page for cut and paste purposes ☺

Cut and paste each image in the correct category.

Sink vs. Float

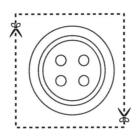

blank page for cut and paste purposes ☺

Magnetic vs. Non Magnetic

Magnets are pieces of metal or rock with an invisible power to attract special kinds of metal. That power is called a **force**. In nature, a force is something that causes a **push or a pull**.

Things that are attracted to magnets are called **magnetic** objects.

 |

magnetic | non - magnetic

blank page for cut and paste purposes ☺

Cut and paste each image in the correct category.

Magnetic vs. Non Magnetic

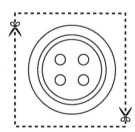

blank page for cut and paste purposes ☺

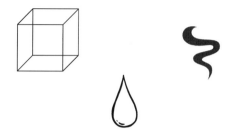

Solid, Liquid and Gas

The three main forms of **matter** are called solids, liquids and gases.

A **solid** keeps its shape. In a solid, the particles fit very closely together.

A **liquid** takes the shape of its container. In a liquid, the particles are still close together but a little further apart in comparison to a solid.

A **gas** fills its container. In gases, the particles are much further apart in comparison to both solids and liquids.

solid

liquid

gas

23

blank page for cut and paste purposes ☺

Cut and paste each image in the correct category.

Solid, Liquid & Gas

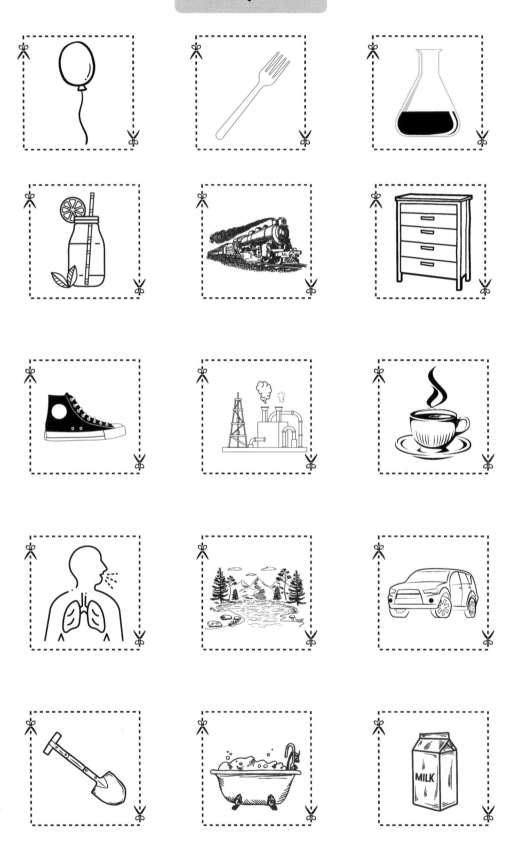

blank page for cut and paste purposes ☺

Human Organs

 The control centre for speech, coordination, memory, thoughts and emotions.

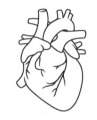 Pumps blood around the body to keep us alive.

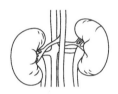 Takes waste out of the blood and makes urine.

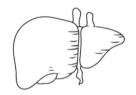 Cleans our blood, produces bile, and stores sugar.

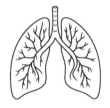 Helps us breathe by taking oxygen in, and sending carbon dioxide out.

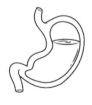 Digests food.

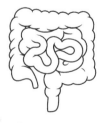 A small and large part that absorbs food and water, and excretes waste.

Color in the organs and trace their names.

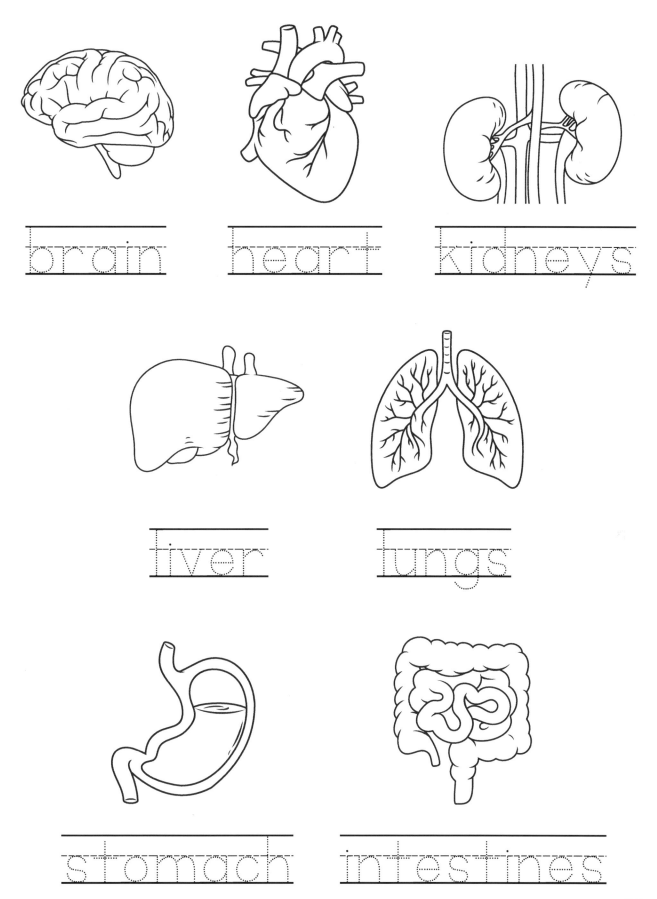

brain

heart

kidneys

liver

lungs

stomach

intestines

26

Color in the organs and write their names.

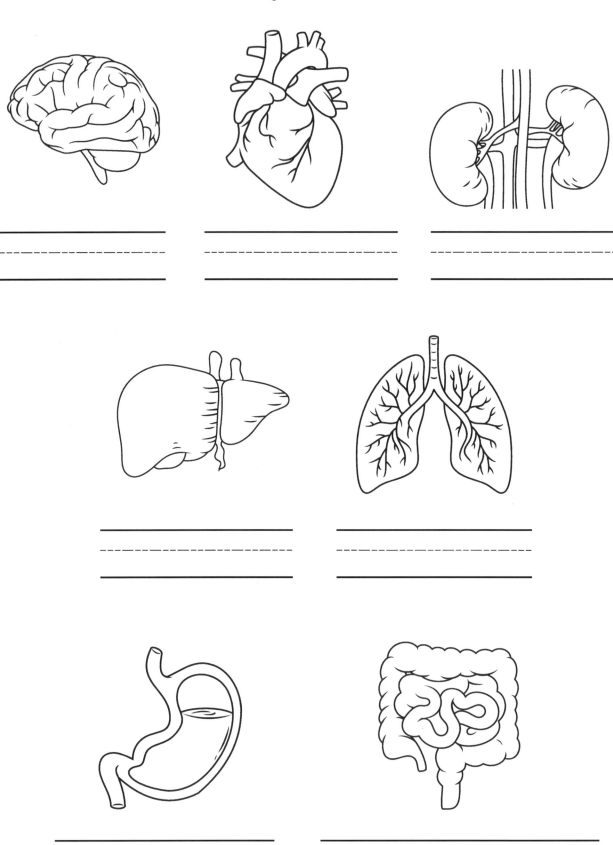

_____   _____   _____
- - - - - - - - -   - - - - - - - - -   - - - - - - - - - - - - - -
_____   _____   _____

_____   _____
- - - - - - - - -   - - - - - - - - -
_____   _____

_____   _____
- - - - - - - - -   - - - - - - - - - - - -
_____   _____

Color in the organs and draw a line to their correct location on the body.

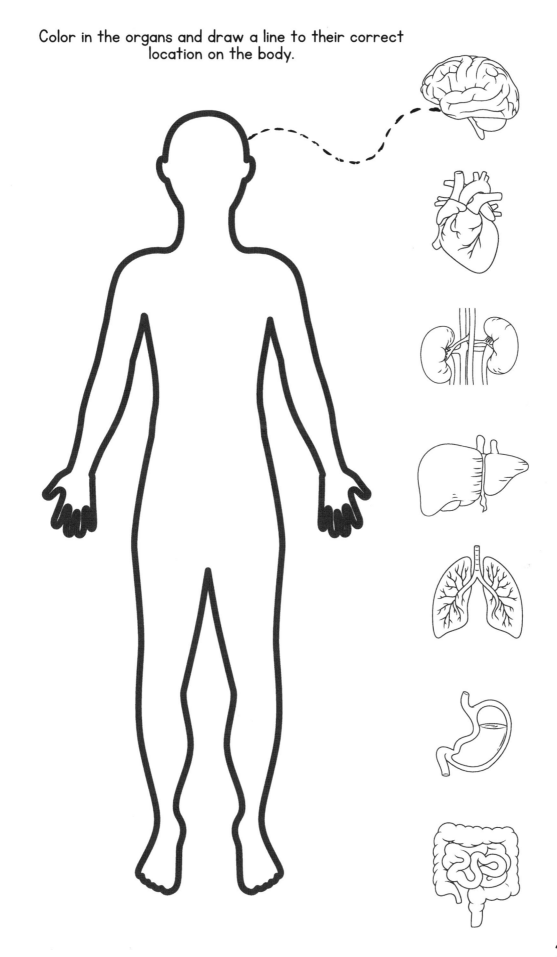

Color in the Planets and trace their names.

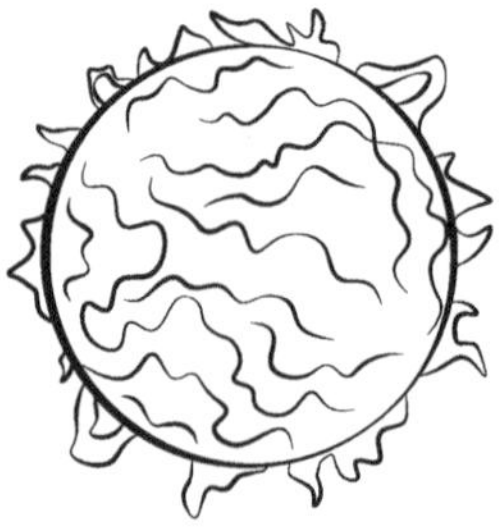

Sun

Mercury

Venus

Earth

Mars

Jupiter

Saturn

Uranus

Neptune

Color in the Planets and write their names.

_____
- - - - - - - - - - - - - - - - -
_____
- - - - - - - - - - - - - - - - -
_____

_____
- - - - - - - - - - - - - - - - -
_____
- - - - - - - - - - - - - - - - -
_____

_____
- - - - - - - - - - - - - - - - -
_____
- - - - - - - - - - - - - - - - -
_____

_____
- - - - - - - - - - - - - - - - -
_____

_____
- - - - - - - - - - - - - - - - -
_____

_____
- - - - - - - - - - - - - - - - -
_____

30

Draw a line to match the planets to their correct names.

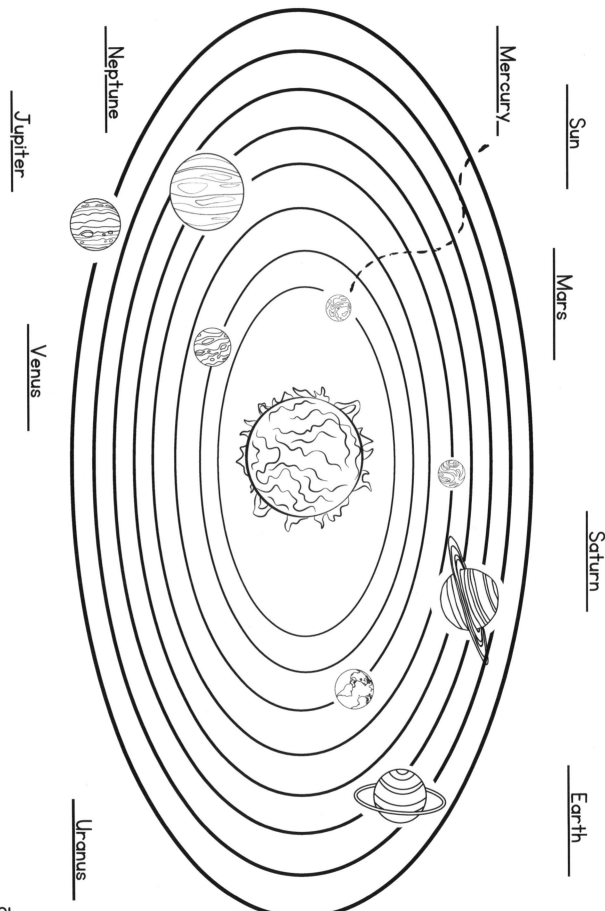

Sun _____

Mercury _____

Mars _____

Saturn _____

Earth _____

Neptune _____

Jupiter _____

Venus _____

Uranus _____

31

Zoology
Butterfly, Frog & Sea Turtle

Books

Monarch Butterfly by Gail Gibson
From Tadpole to Frog by Wendy Pfeffer
One Tiny Turtle by Nicola Davies

Songs

Caterpillar Caterpillar by Kira Willey (yoga version)
Life Cycle of a Butterfly by Jack Hartmann
Butterfly by Nancy Kopman
Frogs Life Cycle by Jack Hartmann
Sea Turtle by Dhruva
Sea Turtle Swish by Jill Gallina

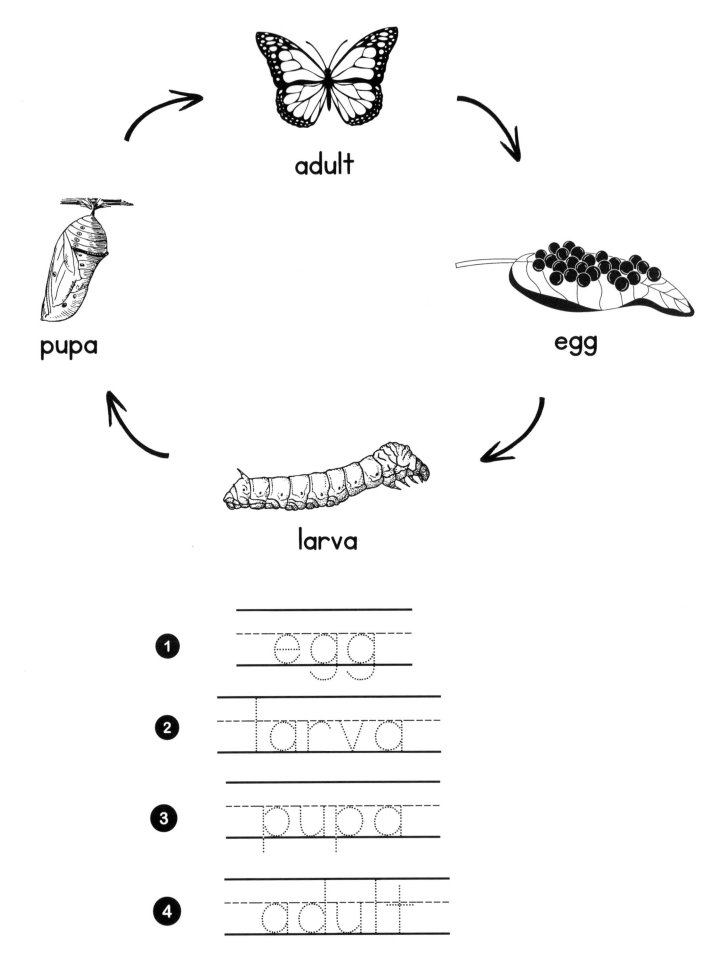

adult

pupa

egg

larva

1 egg

2 larva

3 pupa

4 adult

33

Color in the parts of the butterfly and trace their names.

antennae

head

fore wing

thorax

wing cell

hind wing

wing vein

abdomen

34

Color in the parts of the butterfly and write their names.

_____
- - - - - - - - - - - - - - - - - -

_____
- - - - - - - - - - - - - - - - - -
_____

_____
- - - - - - - - - - - - - - - - - -
_____

_____
- - - - - -

_____
- - - - - - - - - - - - - - - - - -

_____
- - - - - - - - - - - - - - - - - -
_____

_____
- - - - - - - - - - - - - - - - - -
_____

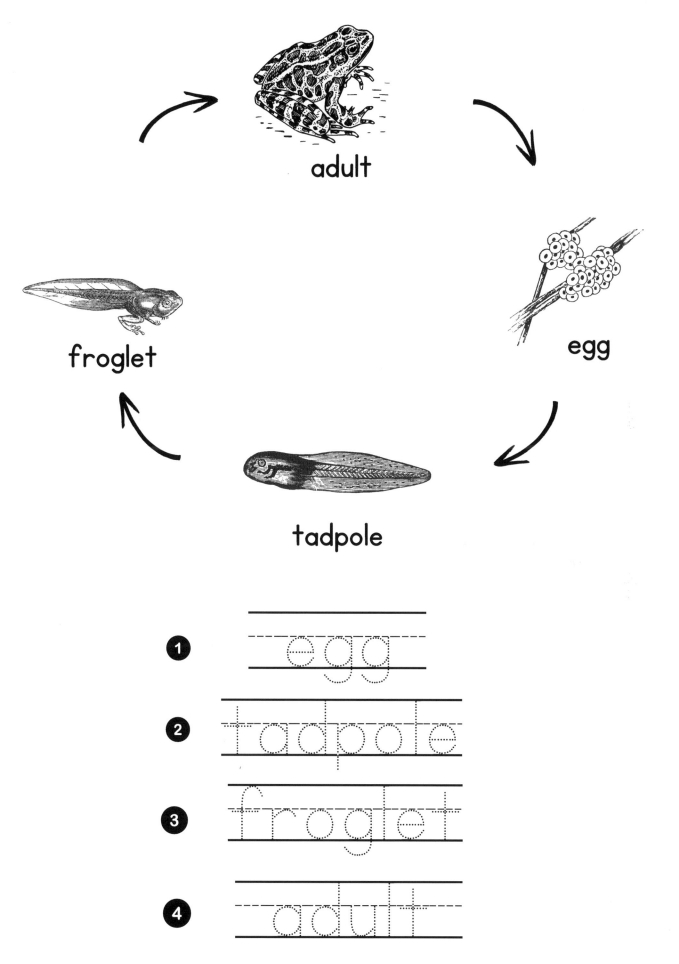

adult

egg

froglet

tadpole

1. egg

2. tadpole

3. froglet

4. adult

36

Color in the parts of the frog and trace their names.

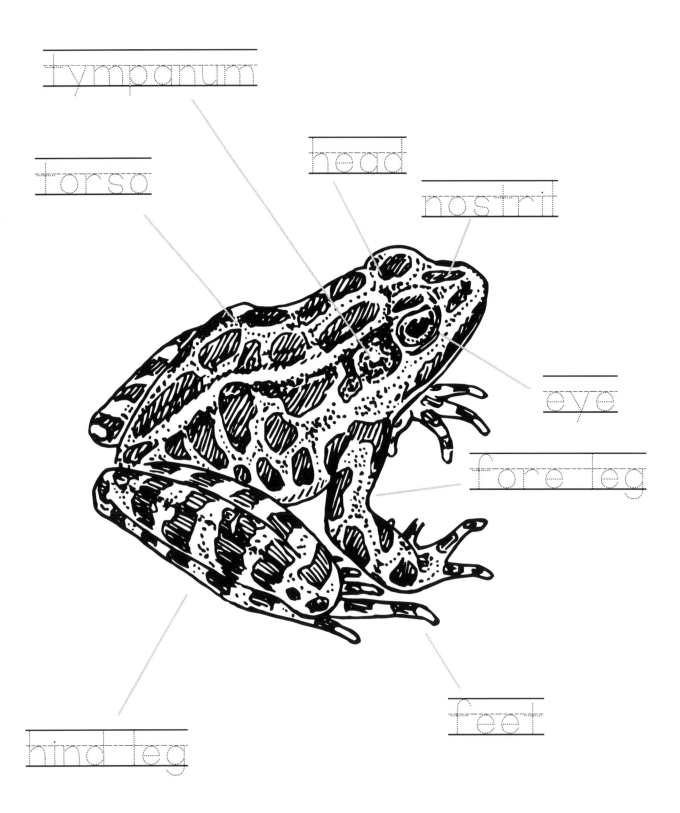

tympanum

torso

head

nostril

eye

fore leg

hind leg

feet

Color in the parts of the frog and write their names.

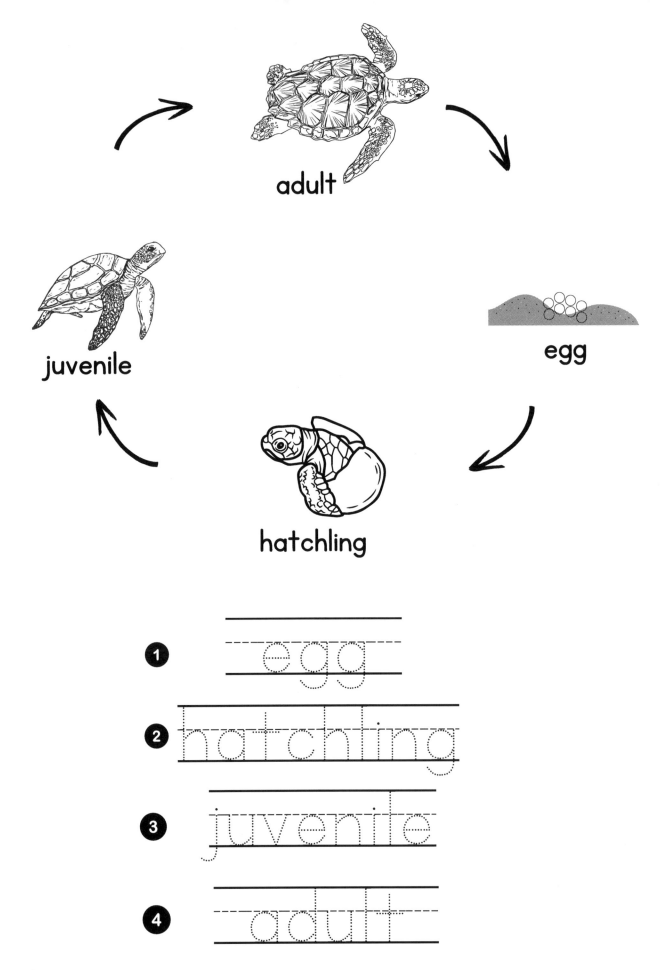

adult

egg

juvenile

hatchling

1 egg

2 hatchling

3 juvenile

4 adult

39

Color in the parts of the turtle and trace their names.

scale

shell

neck

beak

tail

eye

scute

flipper

Color in the parts of the turtle and write their names.

Botany

Tree, Flower & Leaf

<u>Books</u>

From Seed to Plant by Gail Gibbons
The Tiny Seed by Eric Carle
Up in the Garden and Down in the Dirt by Kate Messner
Tap the Magic Tree by Christie Matheson
The Magic and Mystery of Trees by by Claire McElfatrick
A Leaf Can Be . . . by Laura Purdie Salas

<u>Songs</u>

Parts of a Plant by Nancy Kopman
I am a Tree by Nancy Kopman
Under a Shady Tree by The Laurie Berkner Band
Imaging You are a Tree by Kira Willey
Little Seed by Elizabeth Mitchell
Sing a Song of Flowers by The Kiboomers

Color in the different parts of the tree and trace the words.

leaves

branches

trunk

roots

Color in the different parts of the tree and write the words.

_____
- - - - - - - - - - - - -
_____

_____
- - - - - - - - - - - - - - - - - - -
_____

_____
- - - - - - - - - - - - -
_____

_____
- - - - - - - - - - - - - - - - - -
_____

44

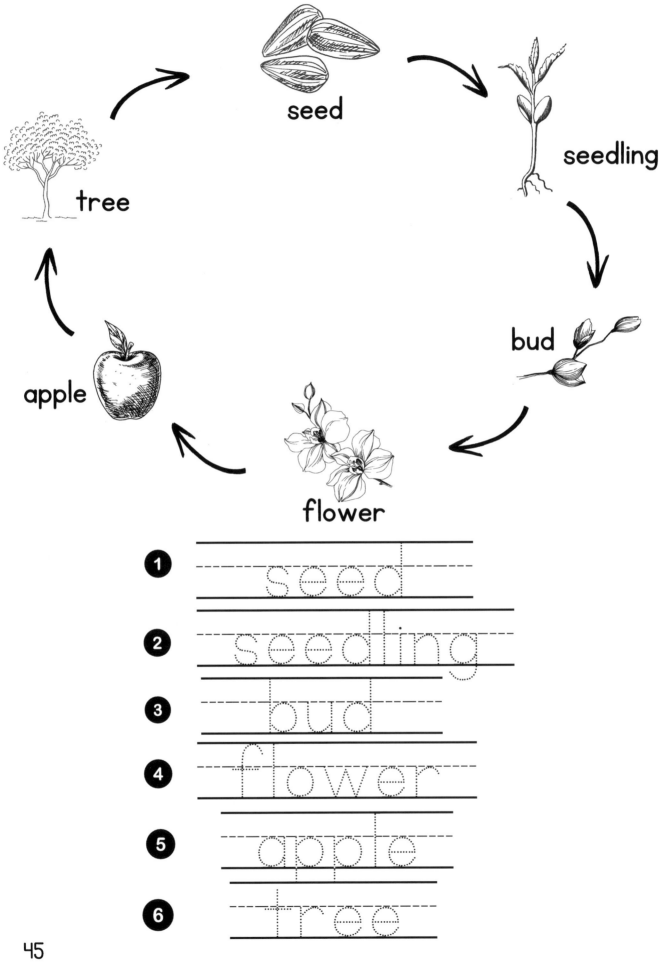

seed

seedling

tree

bud

apple

flower

1 seed

2 seedling

3 bud

4 flower

5 apple

6 tree

45

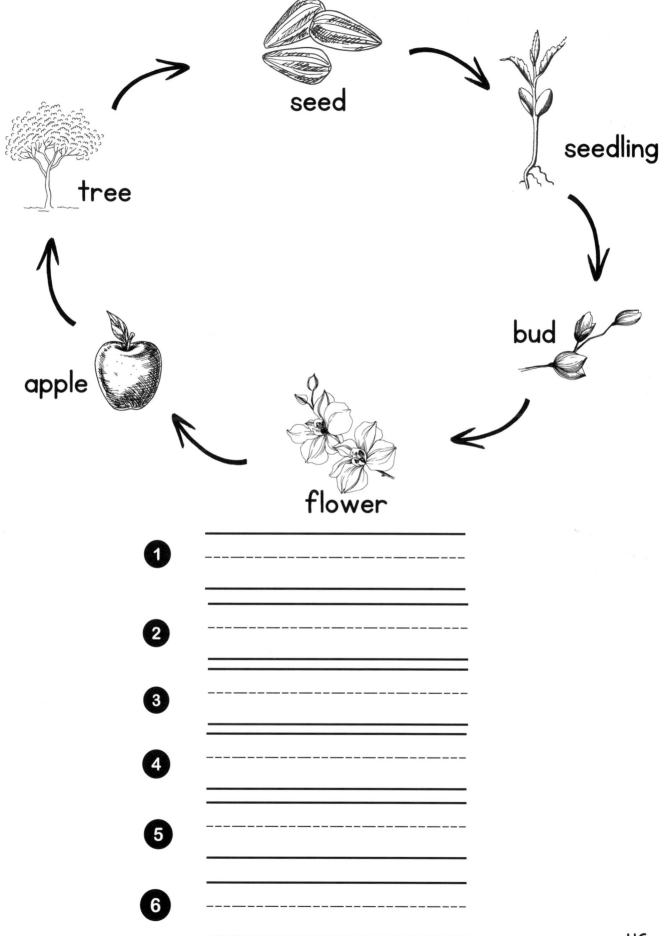

seed

seedling

tree

bud

apple

flower

1

2

3

4

5

6

Color in the different parts of the flower and trace the words.

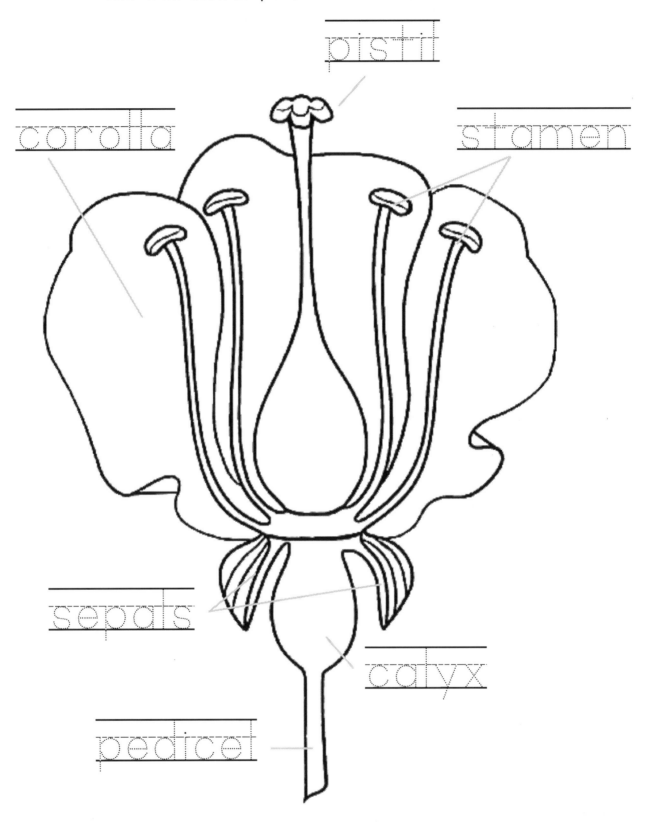

pistil

corolla

stamen

sepals

calyx

pedicel

Color in the different parts of the flower and write the words.

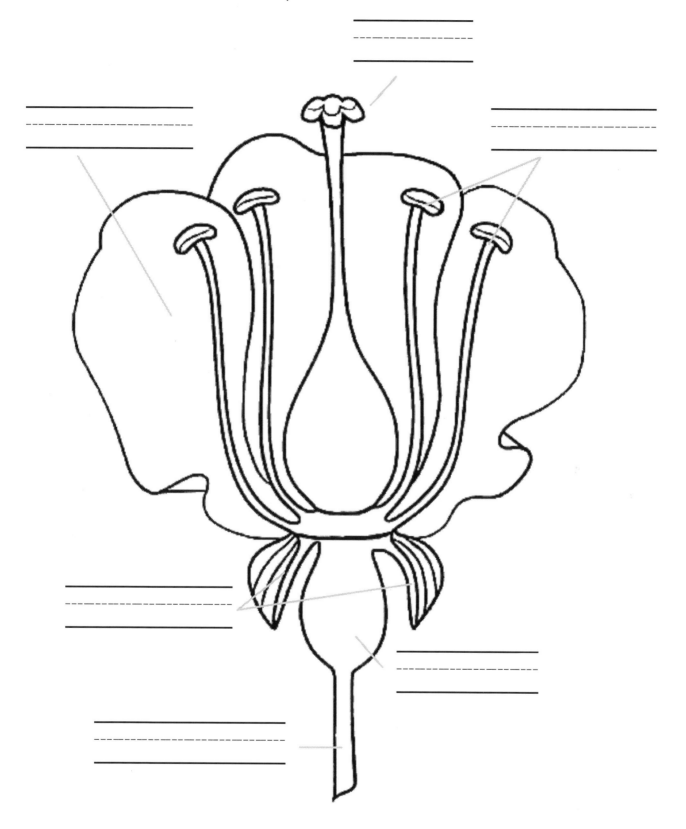

Color in the different types of flowers and trace their names.

hibiscus

waterlily

plumeria

sunflower

pansy

tulip

rose

daffodil

hydrangea

orchid

Color in the different parts of the leaf and trace their names.

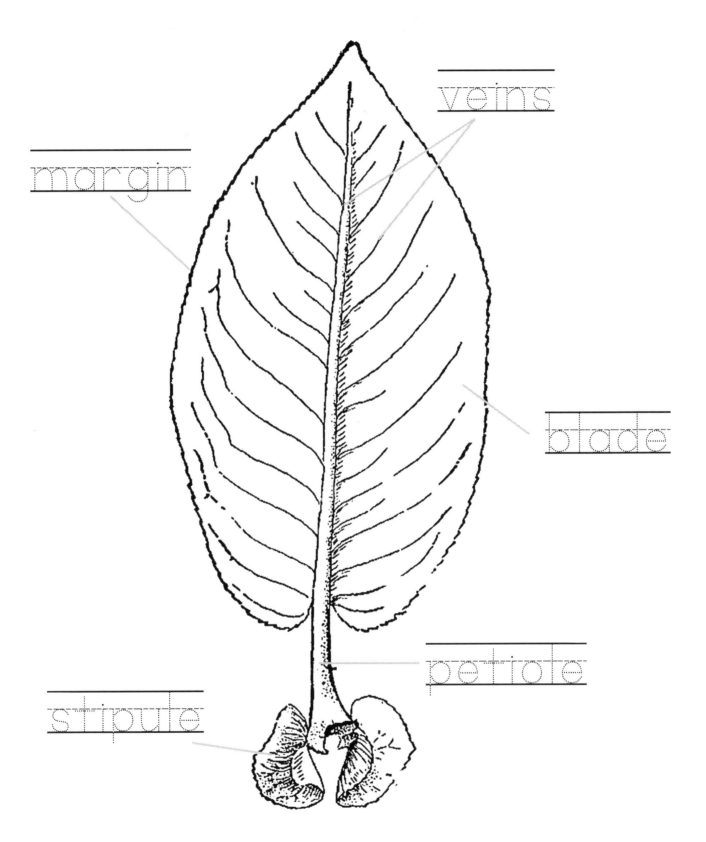

veins

margin

blade

petiole

stipule

51

Color in the different parts of the leaf and write their names.

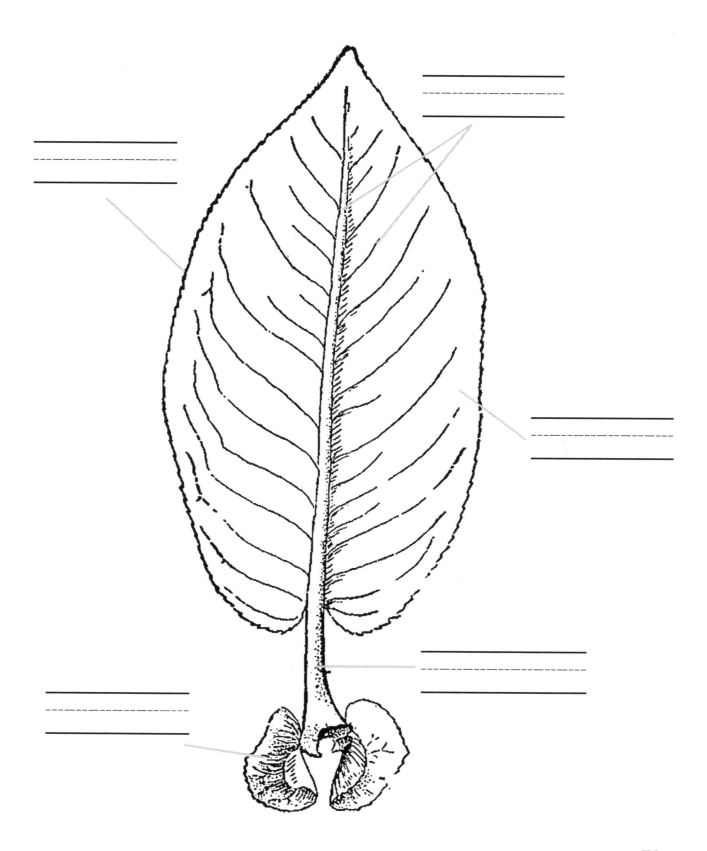

Color in the different types of the leaves and trace their names.

cordate

fan-shaped

lanceolate

sagittate

North America

North America Extensions

Books:

Coqui in the City by Nomar Perez
Redwoods by Jason Chin
Caribbean Dream by Rachel Isadora
Dreamers By Yuyi Morales
Corduroy by Don Freeman
Winged Wonders by Meeg Pincus

Native Musicians

USA: This Land is Your Land by Woody Guthrie
USA: Shine by Sihasin
USA: Can't Help Falling in Love by Elvis Presley
USA: Somethings Got a Hold on Me by Etta James
Canada: My Heart Will Go On by Celine Dion
Canada: If You Could Read My Mind by Gordon Lightfoot
Mexico: Si Nos Dejan by Luis Miguel
Nicaragua: Yo no se Manana by Luis Enrique
Cuba: La Vida es Un Carnaval by Celia Cruz
Puerto Rico: Alexander Hamilton by Lin Manuel Miranda

Landmarks of North America

Chichen Itza

Statue of Liberty

Grand Canyon

Le Chateau Frontenac

56

Color in the animals and trace their names.

bison

cougar

bald eagle

raccoon

moose

Color in the animals and trace their names.

monarch butterfly

manatee

crocodile

axolotl

dart frog

Color in the flags of North America.

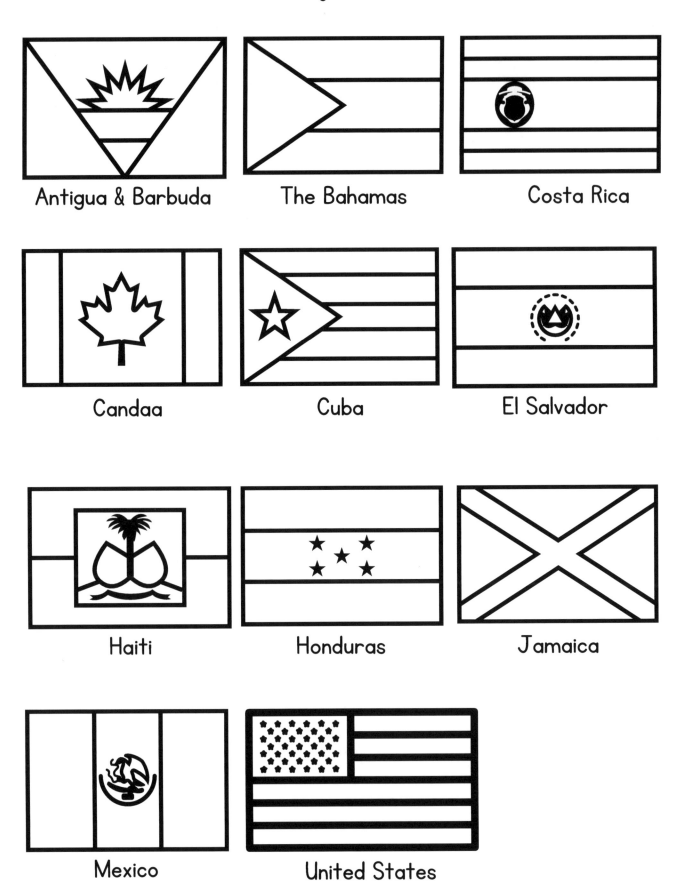

Antigua & Barbuda

The Bahamas

Costa Rica

Candaa

Cuba

El Salvador

Haiti

Honduras

Jamaica

Mexico

United States

59

South America

South America Extensions

Books:

Biblioburro : a true story from Colombia by Jeanette Winter
The magic bean tree : a legend from Argentina by by Nancy Van Laan
"Slowly, slowly, slowly," said the sloth by Eric Carle
Dancing turtle: A folktale from Brazil by Pleasant DeSpain

Children's Songs in Spanish

Buenos Dias by Jose Luis Orozo
Son Los Colores by Janice Buckner
Mi Cuerpo Hace Musica by Sol y Canto
En el Zoologico by Mairim & Marc Musica
Chocolate by Cantare
Rayito Del Sol by Magdalena Fleitas

Native Muscisians

Argentina: Barrio Pobre by Nelly Omar
Colombia: La Tierra Del Olvido by Carlos Vives
Brazil: Deixa A Vida Me Levar by Zeca Pagadinho

Landmarks of South America

Christ the
Redeemer

Machu Picchu

Iguazú Falls

Color in the animals and trace their names.

toucan

sloth

emerald tree boa

anteater

spider monkey

63

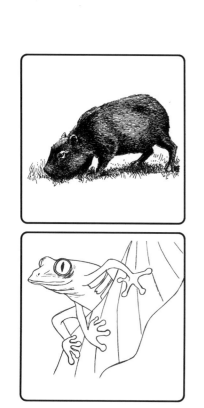

Color in the animals and trace their names.

capybara

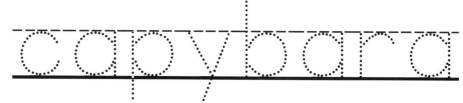

red eyed tree frog

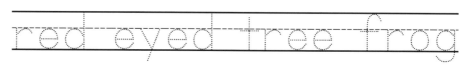

jaguar

caiman

guanaco

Color in the flags of South America.

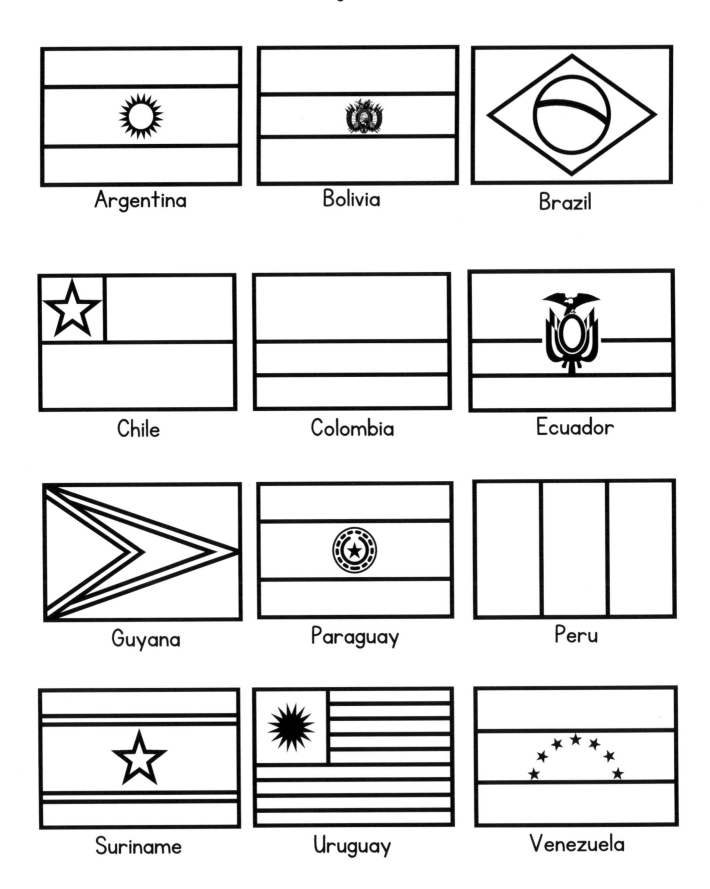

Argentina

Bolivia

Brazil

Chile

Colombia

Ecuador

Guyana

Paraguay

Peru

Suriname

Uruguay

Venezuela

Europe

Europe Extensions

Books:

Building on nature: The life of Antoni Gaudi by Rachel Rodríguez
La La Rose by Satome Ichikawa
Adèle & Simon by Barbara McClintock
A Walk in London by Salvatore Rubbino

Native Musicians

Spain: Volver by Estrella Morente
France: Non, Je Ne Regrette Rien by Edith Pilaf
Germany: 99 Luftballoons by Nena
Italy: O Sole Mio by Luciano Pavarroti
Poland: Nocturne by Frederic Chopin

Landmarks of Europe

Big Ben

Eiffel Tower

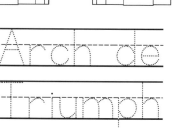

Arch de
Triumph

Leaning Tower
of Pisa

Color in the animals and trace their names.

red fox

lynx

reindeer

rabbit

hedgehog

Color in the animals and trace their names.

brown bear

grey wolf

dormouse

mallard duck

badger

70

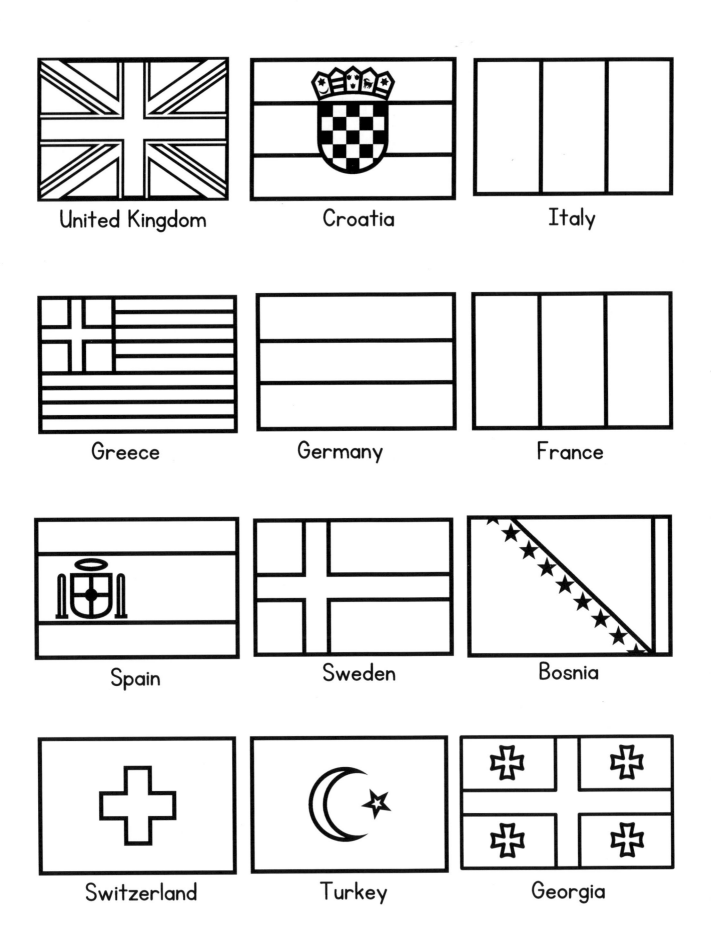

United Kingdom

Croatia

Italy

Greece

Germany

France

Spain

Sweden

Bosnia

Switzerland

Turkey

Georgia

71

Asia

Asia Extensions

Books:

Same, Same, but Different by Jenny Sue Kostecki-Shaw
Elephant in the Dark : Based on a Poem by Rumi by Mina Javaherbin
The Wheels on the Tuk Tuk by Surishtha Sehgal
A gift for Amma : Market Day in India by Meera Sriram
Monsoon Afternoon by Kashmira Sheth

Native Musicians

Japan: Miami Vice Chancellor by Kodo
China: The Butterfly Lovers by Cheng Gang
China(Mongolian Folk): Flowers by Hanggai
Pakistan: Kali Kali Zulfon Ke Phande Na Dalo Nusrat Fateh Ali Khan
India: Baale by Ranjani Gayatri

Landmarks of Asia

Great Wall of China

Taj Mahal

Tian Tan Buddha

Mount Fuji

Color in the animals and trace their names.

panda

komodo dragon

orangutan

red panda

sun bear

Color in the animals and trace their names.

bactrian camel

pangolin

elephant

tiger

leopard

Color in the flags of Asia.

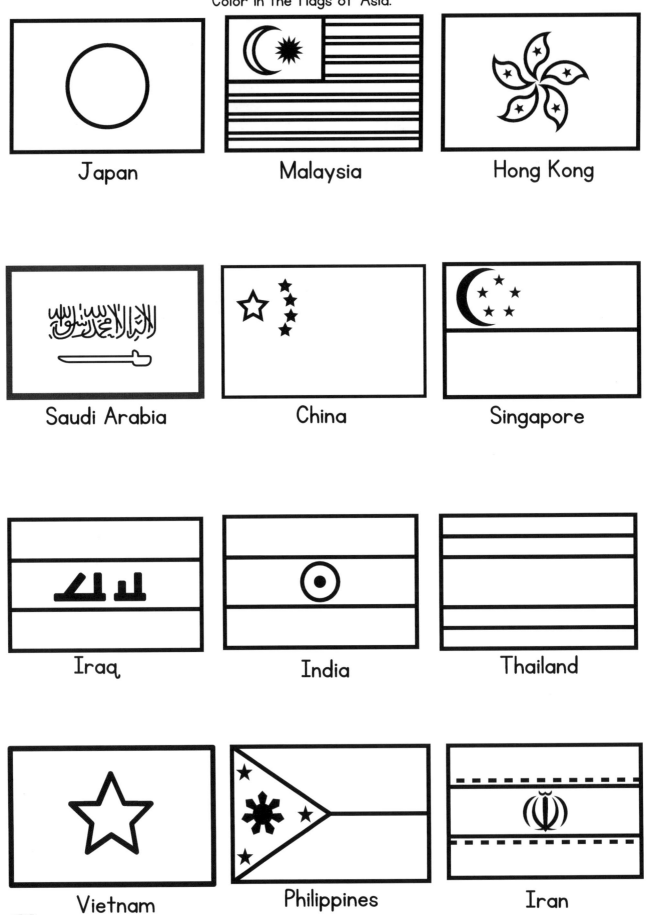

Japan

Malaysia

Hong Kong

Saudi Arabia

China

Singapore

Iraq

India

Thailand

Vietnam

Philippines

Iran

77

Australia

Australia Extensions
*includes Oceania

Books:

My Ocean Home Fiji by Penelope Casey
Hello Mama Wallaroo by Darrin Lunde
Elizabeth, Queen of the Seas byr Lynne Cox
D is for Down Under by Devin Scillian

Native Musicians

Australia: Gday G day by Slim Dusty
Papua New Guinea: Abebe by George Telek
New Zealand: The Haka by Maori Tribe
Tahiti: Te Pua Noanoa by Toa Reva

Landmarks of Australia

Sydney Opera House

Sydney Harbour Bridge

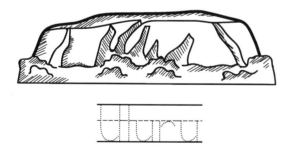

Uluru

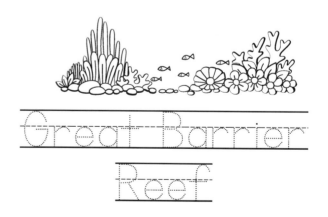

Great Barrier Reef

Color in the animals and trace their names.

koala

wombt

kangaroo

platypus

dingo

Color in the animals and trace their names.

tasmanian devil

kookaburra

emu

frilled-necked lizard

echidnas

Color in the flags of Australia.

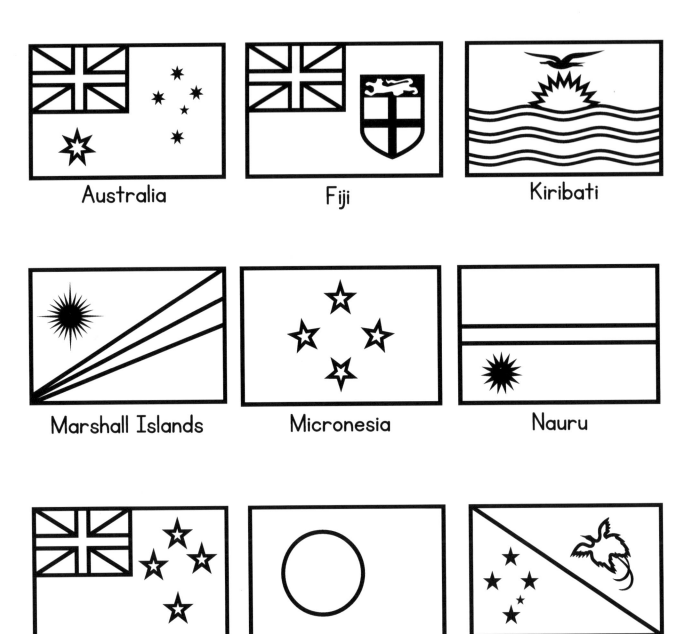

Australia   Fiji   Kiribati

Marshall Islands   Micronesia   Nauru

New Zealand   Palau   Papua New Guineau

Antarctica

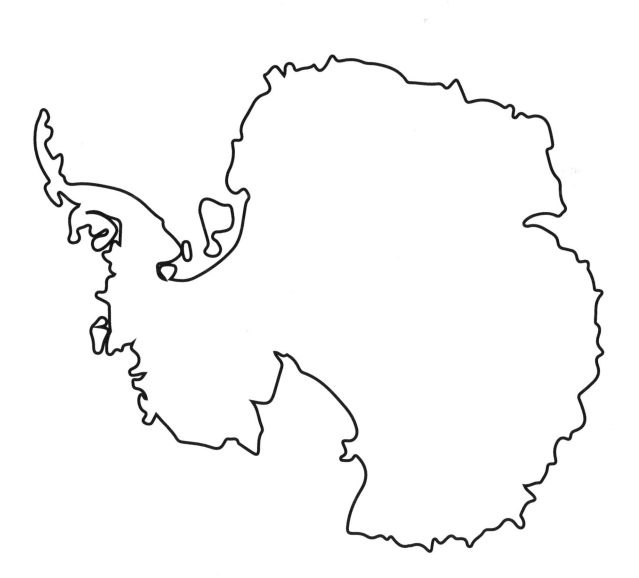

Antarctica Extensions
*includes Arctic

Books:

North Pole South Pole by Nancy Smiler Levinson Read-aloud
Antarctica by Helen Cowcher
One Day on Our Blue Planet in the Antarctic by Ella Bailey
Where is Home, Little Pip by Karma Wilson
A Trip To The Bottom Of The World With Mouse by Frank Viva

Local Music

Antarctica Music From the Ice by Cheryl E Leonard
Ocean Memories by Terje Isungset

Color in the animals and trace their names.

rockhopper penguin

orca

albatross

blue whale

elephant seal

Color in the animals and trace their names.

polar bear

arctic hare

husky

caribou

walrus

Africa

Africa Extensions

Books:

Bintou's Braids by Sylviane A. Diouf
Deep in the Sahara by Kelly Cunnane
The Wooden Camel by Wanuri Kahiu
Water Hole Waiting by Jane Kurtz

Native Muscisians

Algeria: Sbabi by Khlaed
Nigeria: Sele Yi Leju by King Sunny Ade
Congo: BOH Africa by Zaiko Langa Langa
Mali: Ai Du by Ali Farka Toure
Morocco: The Fire Within by Hassan Hakmoun
South Africa: Mbube by Mahotella Queens

Color in the animals and trace their names.

zebra

giraffe

lion

aardvark

hippopotamus

Color in the animals and trace their names.

baboon

elephant

rhinoceros

wildebeest

gazelle

Color in the flags of Africa.

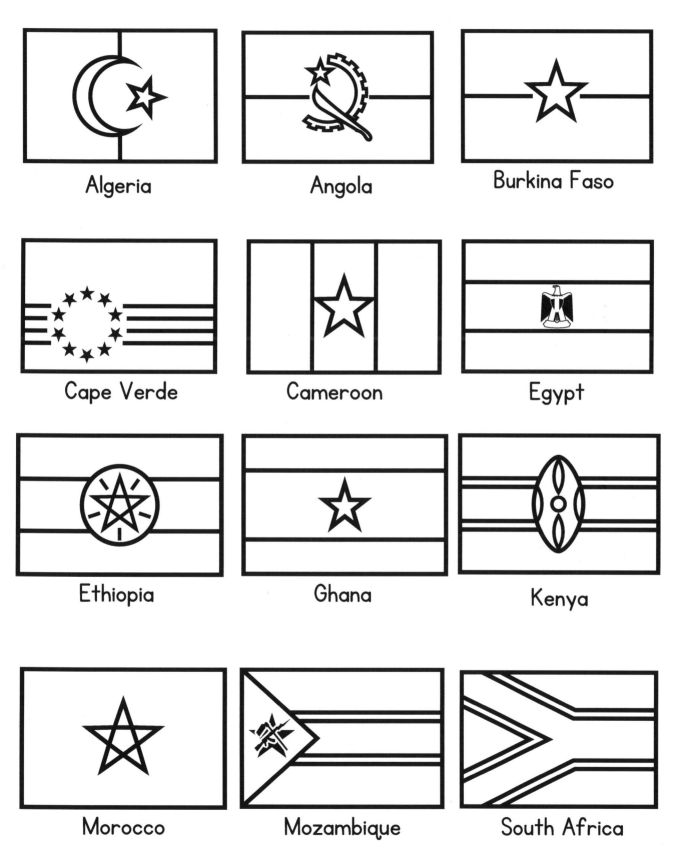

Algeria

Angola

Burkina Faso

Cape Verde

Cameroon

Egypt

Ethiopia

Ghana

Kenya

Morocco

Mozambique

South Africa

Made in the USA
Coppell, TX
07 September 2023